Kursk

by

Christopher Chant

Colour Illustrations by

Keith Ward

ALMARK

ALMARK PUBLISHING CO. LTD., LONDON

First published October, 1975

ISBN 0 85524 236 1 (paper cover)
ISBN 0 85524 237 X (case bound)

Photoset by Seventy Set Ltd, London
Printed in Great Britain by
Panlitho Ltd.,
The Highway, London E1
for the publishers, Almark Publishing Co. Ltd.,
49 Malden Way, New Malden,
Surrey KT3 6EA, England

CONTENTS

SOURCES

Carell P.   *The Scorched Earth*
Chainey O.   *Zhukov*
Golikov   *Kursk*
Guderian H.   *Panzer Leader*
Icks R. J.   *Famous Tank Battles*
Jukes G.   *Kursk*
Klink E.   *Das Gesetz des Handelns "Zita-delle"*

Mackintosh M.   *Juggernaut*
Manstein E.   *Lost Victories*
Seaton A.   *The Russo German War*
Solovyov B.   *The Battle of Kursk*
Zhukov G.   *The Memoirs of Marshal Zhukov*

Soviet T34s group for an attack.

1. Hitler's Decision

History has yet to accord the Battle of Kursk a place worthy of its supreme importance during World War II. The battle was the largest armoured clash that has to date occurred, but the turning point in Germany's war against Soviet Russia is still reckoned to be the great defeat at Stalingrad during January and February 1942. But although the surrender of the starved and frozen remnants of the German 6th Army in Stalingrad was undoubtedly an event of great significance, it must be remembered that Germany did manage to recover sufficiently to launch one more major offensive against the Russians on the Eastern Front – the great pincer offensive against the Soviet forces holding the Kursk salient in July 1943. After the defeat at Kursk a Russian offensive followed which put the strategic initiative in the East totally into Russia's hands. From this time onwards Germany could merely try to hold back the mighty westward blows launched periodically by the Red Army. The defeat at Stalingrad signalled what lay ahead for Germany, but the defeat at Kursk (a defeat that at one time hung on the knife-edge of victory) made the final extinction of the Third Reich a certainty.

Three weeks before the surrender of the last elements of the 6th Army cut off in Stalingrad, the Red Army launched a major offensive on January 12, 1943 from the line of the Don river in the direction of the Donets and beyond. By March 1 the reeling Axis forces had been pushed back behind the Donets from Slavyansk to Belgorod, and the vital town of Kharkov had fallen to the Russians. Further north still, the Russians had taken the great town of Kursk, and pushed forward in a salient south of the German-held city of Orel. The German position looked extremely serious, but the Russian advance was halted and thrown back finally to the south of Kursk in one of the most remarkable counter-offensives of the war by Field-Marshal Erich von Manstein's Army Group 'South'. Although outnumbered by over five to one, Manstein's forces wiped out the salient between Zmiyev and Slavyansk towards Dnepropetrovsk between February 19 and March 1, and that between Zmiyev and Belgorod towards Akhtyrka between March 1 and 25, in the process retaking

Kharkov. Thus the Russian forces held the line of the Donets and Mius rivers south of Belgorod, and a great salient 160 miles across and 80 miles deep centred around Kursk. The spring thaw finally halted operations on both sides at the end of March, giving weary troops the chance to rest, and their commanders time to plan their next moves.

What was Germany to do? The Oberkommando der Wehrmacht (OKW or Armed Forces High Command), which ran the German war effort in all theatres save Russia, proposed a strategic defensive allowing forces to be moved to the West to meet the expected Allied landings now inevitable after the final defeat of the Axis forces in North Africa. The Oberkommando des Heeres (OKH or Army High Command), which ran the war against Russia under Hitler's overall supervision, agreed that a strategic defensive was necessary, but only after a major local offensive to spoil any Russian plans for a summer offensive. Hitler agreed, with the extra reasons that he needed a major victory to strengthen the failing resolve of several of Germany's satellites, notably Finland and Rumania. Hitler and General Kurt Zeitzler, the OKH chief-of-staff, agreed that a limited offensive should be undertaken at the time of the dry period that followed the thaw, in April, and that this could be completed in time to redeploy any forces that might be necessary to meet an Allied landing on the European continent. But where was the limited offensive desirable on military and political grounds to be struck? The obvious answer was the Russian salient that jutted out into German-held Russia around Kursk.

The problem with the Kursk salient, however, was that it was so obvious a place against which to launch such a blow that the Russian high command or Stavka must see this and pour in reinforcements. Therefore speed was essential, and preparations made as quickly as possible. But time was squandered thoughtlessly by Hitler and his planning officers. Initial work on the plans for the offensive, now code-named 'Zitadelle' or 'Citadel', began early in March, before the final outcome of the battles that finalised the shape of the salient had been determined, with the intention that the offensive be launched in April. This would give the Russians little time to set in hand a massive reinforcement programme. Now reasons for delay began to pour in: troops could not be moved up to their start lines in sufficient time; and Field-Marshal Walter Model, whose 9th Army was to make up the northern of the two pincers to be used in pinching out the salient, and in whose judgement Hitler placed great faith, declared that the forces allotted to him were sufficient in neither numbers nor quality to achieve their objectives. The provisional date in the middle of April first intended for the offensive passed without a protest.

On May 4 Hitler summoned a meeting to discuss the matter. Amongst those present were Hitler himself, Zeitzler, Manstein (whose Army Group 'South' was to provide the forces for the southern pincer in the form of the 4th Panzerarmee [Panzer army] and Operational Group 'Kempf'), Field-Marshal Günter von Kluge (whose Army Group 'Centre' included the 9th Army) and Colonel-General Heinz Guderian, recently recalled from retirement to take up the post of Inspector-General of Armoured Forces. Model himself was represented by a letter in which he called for further postponement, and otherwise left his readers in little doubt that he thought the offensive doomed to failure because of the strength of the Soviet defences. Kluge and Manstein were in favour of pressing on with Zitadelle, but only if it could be launched in the very near future, before further Russian forces moved into the salient. Guderian was totally against the plan, considering that it would waste the resources of new tanks just beginning to flow from the factories. Field-Marshal Wilhelm Keitel, head of the OKW, favoured the attack; General Alfred Jodl, chief of the Armed Forces Operational Staff or Wehrmachtführungstab, was against it. Even Hitler himself now had doubts, but finally decided that the offensive should be launched – but only after more of the new Panther and Tiger tanks and Ferdinand (or Elefant) self-propelled guns had become available. Production of these new weapons was still slow, however, and many defects had still to be ironed out. Guderian, in particular, realised that the tactical utility of the new vehicles would be much reduced by their defects, and that the vehicles on which the new armoured divisions might have been built up would inevitably be lost. But Hitler was mesmerised by the idea of his new weapons destroying all before them, and would not relent.

Although he admitted that the thought of the offensive terrified him, Hitler insisted that it go ahead, with the most stringent security precautions being enforced to prevent the Russians from finding out the nature, timing and location of the planned attack. At a final conference on July 1, attended by commanders down to corps level who would be involved in the offensive, Hitler once again repeated his determination to retreat no further, and that it was merely the inefficiency and pusillanimity of Germany's allies that had caused previous setbacks. From now onwards Germany would hold everywhere, and the forthcoming attack's success was essential towards this end. The date was fixed for the start of the great battle – July 4 in the south and July 5 in the north.

Hitler and all his commanders knew that Zitadelle was very much a gamble – a gamble that could only come off if the enemy were in total ignorance of the German intentions. Enormous effort went into camouflaging the German preparations at the front, but so massive a concentration of men and matériel could not be completely concealed, and Russian front-line commanders realised that an attack was imminent and made preparations to counter it.

Far more important, however, was the fact that the Stavka was kept fully informed of the German plans by the 'Lucy' spy ring. This fascinating network, headed by Rudolf Rössler in Switzerland, played a crucial part in the war; indeed, had Stalin heeded the ring's warning about the German invasion of June 1941, the course of the war would have been significantly different. By the time of Zitadelle, however, the ring's reports were accepted fully, and proved decisive in the Russian planning to meet the German offensive. From a primary source, whose identity has never been discovered but who must have held a position high in German army circles, Rössler received full information of the German plans and forces; this Rössler forwarded to Moscow, allowing the planners there to dispose their forces in the right places to meet the German threat, and build up the most massive system of field fortifications the world has seen.

One of Hitler's and Zeitzler's justifications for the continued existence of Zitadelle had been the need to disrupt Russian preparations for their next offensive, which the Germans thought would take place the following winter. The Russians, however, were planning a major summer offensive to eliminate the two German salients centred on Orel and Kharkov, to the north and south respectively of the Kursk salient. With little alteration these plans could be used to check the German effort at Kursk, which in turn would ease the tasks of the Soviet forces pinching out the German salients: the 'Fascist' forces would be allowed to batter at the shoulders of the Kursk salient, exhausting themselves and losing considerable quantities of men and matériel in the process. When the Germans were exhausted, the Russians would launch large counter-offensives to the north and south of the Kursk salient and roll back the hapless Germans along a wide front. Nevertheless, the Stavka did not underestimate the skill and determination of the German army, and massed very considerable forces both in and behind the salient to hold the German attacks.

The importance attached to the defence of the Kursk salient by the Russians is attested by the attachment to the forces in the area as Stavka representatives of Marshals of the Soviet Union Aleksandr Vasilevsky and Georgi Zhukov, the latter the most distinguished commander yet produced by Soviet Russia.

The terrain of the Kursk salient is for the most part low rolling hills of basically sandy soil, dotted with small farming communities along the numerous rivers, orchards and sunflower fields – all in all excellent country for armoured forces.

Russian front-line commanders were warned of the imminence of a German onslaught on July 2. Two days later a German deserter informed them that the attack was due at any moment. Although they had no inkling of it, the Germans would achieve none of the strategic surprise on which their plans so depended. All they could hope for was an element of tactical surprise.

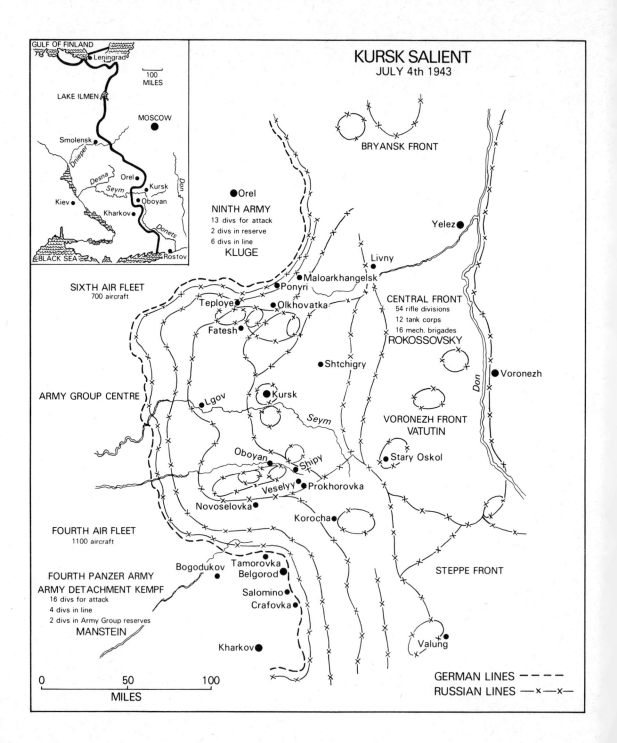

KURSK SALIENT
JULY 4th 1943

GULF OF FINLAND
Leningrad
100 MILES
Lake ILMEN
MOSCOW
Smolensk
Dnieper
Desna
Orel
Kursk
Seym
Oboyan
Don
Kiev
Kharkov
Donets
BLACK SEA
Rostov

BRYANSK FRONT

Orel

NINTH ARMY
13 divs for attack
2 divs in reserve
6 divs in line
KLUGE

Yelez

Livny

SIXTH AIR FLEET
700 aircraft

Maloarkhangelsk

Ponyri

Teploye

Olkhovatka

CENTRAL FRONT
54 rifle divisions
12 tank corps
16 mech. brigades
ROKOSSOVSKY

Fatesh

Shtchigry

Voronezh

ARMY GROUP CENTRE

Lgov

Kursk

Seym

VORONEZH FRONT
VATUTIN

Don

Oboyan

Shipy

Stary Oskol

Veselyy

Prokhorovka

Novoselovka

Korocha

FOURTH AIR FLEET
1100 aircraft

STEPPE FRONT

FOURTH PANZER ARMY
ARMY DETACHMENT KEMPF
16 divs for attack
4 divs in line
2 divs in Army Group reserves
MANSTEIN

Bogodukov

Tamorovka
Belgorod

Salomino

Crafovka

Valung

Kharkov

0   50   100
MILES

GERMAN LINES ----
RUSSIAN LINES -x-x-

2. The Forces and Their Plans

In essence the German plan to take the Kursk salient used the same tried and tested pincer attack that had proved so successful against Russian forces since the launching of Operation 'Barbarossa' in June 1941: in the north the 9th Army, heavily reinforced by Panzer forces, would strike down from south of Orel through Ponyri to Kursk; in the south the 4th Panzerarmee, shielded on its eastern flank by Operational Group 'Kempf', would advance from north of Kharkov through Oboyan to meet the 9th Army at Kursk; the Russian forces trapped in the pocket so formed would then be destroyed piecemeal. Kursk would have been retaken, a shorter front line would have been established, and the surplus forces could be despatched to the West.

It was a good, workmanlike plan, based on the tactics that had proved successful before. Unfortunately for the Germans, however, it had three defects: it was stereotyped, and so the Russians knew what to expect; the Russian spy network had revealed the plan to the enemy; and thirdly, the Germans were outnumbered in men, tanks, guns and aircraft by their opponents, who also had the advantage of the commanding ground and prepared defensive positions.

The plan may best be summarised in the words of Operation Order Number 6, signed by Hitler on April 15:

'I have decided to launch Operation "Citadel", the first of this year's offensives, as soon as the weather allows it.

'This attack, therefore, is of vital importance. It must succeed both rapidly and totally. It must give us the initiative for spring and summer. For this reason all the preparations must be carried out with the utmost care and energy. The best formations, the best weapons, the best commanders and considerable quantities of ammunition must be used at the key points. Every commander, every man must be totally convinced of the decisive importance of this offensive. The victory at Kursk must be a beacon to the world.

'I therefore order:

'1. The objective of the offensive is to encircle the

enemy in the Kursk area by the use of heavily concentrated, merciless and fast thrusts by one offensive army each from the regions of Belgorod and south of Orel, and to annihilate them in a pincer attack . . . .

'2. It is vital

(a) to preserve the element of surprise as far as is possible, and especially to keep the enemy guessing about the timing of the offensive; . . .

(b) to concentrate the attacking forces into as narrow a front as possible in order to break through in one step; . . .

(c) to keep the front-line wedges supplied with forces from the rear as quickly as possible to cover their flanks, so that the assault wedges need drive only forwards; . . .

'3. Army Group "South" will jump off with strongly concentrated forces from the line Belgorod-Tomarovka, break through along the line Prilepy-Oboyan, and link up with the attacking army of Army Group "Centre" in and east of Kursk. [To cover the main force's eastern flank] the line Nezhega - Korocha - Skorodnoye - Tim must be reached as quickly as possible . . . . [To cover the main force's western flank] secondary forces are to be used. These will drive into the pocket with the main force as the pocket is formed.

'4. Army Group "Centre" will jump off with its attacking army from the line Trosna-north of Maloarchangelsk after the heaviest concentration of forces, break through along the line Fatezh-Vereytenovo, with its main effort on the eastern flank, and join up with the attacking army of Army Group "South" in and east of Kursk. [To cover the main force's western flank] secondary forces are to be used . . . .

'5. The deployment of both army groups' forces must take place far from the start line under cover of all possible camouflage, blinds and other deceptive measures in such a way that from 28 April the offensive can be launched six days after notification from OKH . . . . The forward movement to the start-line must only occur at night and under the strictest camouflage precautions . . . .

'7. To make sure of security, these plans are to be vouchsafed only to those who absolutely need to know of them. Briefing is to be done as late as possible, and then only phase by phase. At this juncture we must ensure at all costs that no part of our plans leaks out through carelessness or negligence. Enemy intelligence activities must be checked by an enhanced counter-intelligence effort . . . .

'12. The ultimate objectives of the complete operation are:

(a) the movement of the boundary between Army Groups "South" and "Centre" basically to the line Konotop ("South")-Kursk ("South")-Dolgoye ("Centre");

(b) the transfer of the 2nd Army headquarters, with three corps headquarters and nine infantry divisions, as well as other army troops yet to be determined, from Army Group "Centre" to Army Group "South";

(c) the deployment of three other infantry divisions from Army Group "Centre" so that they may be available to OKH north-west of Kursk; and

(d) the withdrawal of all armoured formations from this front for deployment in other theatres . . . .'

For this last major offensive effort in the East the Germans had amassed considerable striking forces. In the north Model's 9th Army of Army Group 'Centre' consisted of General J. Friessner's XXIII Corps on the left, General J. Harpe's XLI Panzer Corps, General J. Lemelsen's XLVII Panzer Corps, General H. Zorn's XLVI Panzer Corps, and General R. Freiherr von Roman's XX Corps on the right. Model's army reserve consisted of Gruppe 'von Esebeck'. Under his command Model had a total of 21 divisions: one Panzergrenadier, six Panzer and 14 infantry. Of the last only eight had been allocated to the Zitadelle offensive. The 9th Army could put over 900 tanks, most of them obsolete Pzkw II and III and obsolescent Pzkw IV vehicles, into the fray. Model's air support was furnished by the 1st Fliegerdivision (Air Division) of the 6th Luftflotte (Air Fleet), with some 730 aircraft. Model's left flank, to the east and north of

Orel, was protected by the divisions of the 2nd Panzerarmee, which despite its designation had lost all its armoured formations to the 9th Army.

To the south of the salient Manstein's main striking force consisted of Colonel-General H. Hoth's 4th Panzerarmee. On its left this had General E. Ott's LII Corps on the left, General O. von Knobelsdorff's XLVIII Panzer Corps in the centre, and SS Gruppenführer (General) P. Hausser's II SS Panzer Corps on the right. South of Belgorod was the Operational Group commanded by General W. Kempf: General H. Breith's III Panzer Corps on the left, Lieutenant-General E. Raus's XI Corps (sometimes referred to as Corps 'Raus') in the centre, and General F. Mattenklott's XLII Corps on the right. Manstein had under his command 22 divisions: two Panzergrenadier, nine Panzer and 11 infantry, including the army group reserve (General W. Nehring's XXIV Panzer Corps). Of his 11 infantry divisions, however, Manstein allotted only seven to Zitadelle. Air support for the southern half of the German pincer was provided by the 1,100 aircraft of VIII Fliegerkorps (Air Corps). The 4th Panzerarmee and Operational Group 'Kempf' could between them muster some 1,000 tanks and 150 assault guns, the total including 200 of the new Panther and 94 of the new Tiger tanks.

The front between the two offensive arms of the pincer, along the western edge of the salient, was held by the seven infantry divisions of the 2nd Army. Little was expected to happen here. It is worth noting that most of the German divisions had been greatly reduced in strength as a result of losses during the spring retreats. By the beginning of the Battle of Kursk, only three Panzergrenadier, 15 Panzer and 15 infantry divisions had been restored to strength – basically those allotted major tasks in Zitadelle. By the same date, of the 3,700 armoured fighting vehicles (including about 500 obsolete vehicles), some 2,500 were allocated to the Zitadelle offensive. Of these, Hitler expected much of the three new vehicles, the Panther medium tank, the Tiger heavy tank, and the Ferdinand tank-hunter. These vehicles were all well-armed (the Panther with a 7.5-cm gun and the others with 8.8-cm weapons), and had basically good armour protection. The

Ferdinand lacked a defensive machine gun, however, allowing Russian infantry and guns to engage it on its more vulnerable flanks and rear. And the Maybach engines of the Tigers and Ferdinands required the skilled driving, that was not readily available amongst front-line troops, to prevent them breaking down. Finally, the Panther was as yet very underdeveloped and unreliable, and showed an alarming tendency to catch fire. The over-hasty introduction of these vehicles, therefore, was to lead to the situation all too correctly feared by Guderian.

Finally, how many guns were available to the Germans? According to Russian sources, on July 5 Model had 6,000 guns and mortars, and Manstein 4,000 similar weapons. These were in themselves sound enough weapons, but the Germans lacked the necessary towing vehicles to give them the type of mobility that was to be needed in the Battle of Kursk.

What of German tactics for the battle? The constant delays in the execution of the basic plan had given commanders time to consider their approaches to the conflict in depth, and to train their troops accordingly, and two totally different types of tactics emerged. The Germans prepared for the offensive with great thoroughness, and all the troops were more than adequately prepared for their tasks. Nonetheless Model and Manstein evolved different offensive tactics for their forces. Model's men, with an adequate proportion of infantry to armour, would attempt to open the way for the armour by the use of conventional infantry/pioneer/artillery tactics. Manstein, on the other hand, felt that he did not have the infantry to be able to afford these steady, but costly, tactics, and therefore evolved what came to be known as the Panzerkeil (armoured wedge). This was a triangular formation of a Tiger or Panther leading, with Pzkw III or IV tanks supporting slightly to the rear and on each flank. The concept was sound, but the composition was not, for though the Panther or Tiger had guns capable of excellent long-range fire, the Russian T-34 and KV-1 tanks would close to short ranges where they could do the German tanks equal damage. During the battle Manstein realised that his tactics were wrong, and ordered that the older tanks lead, to flush the Russian tanks and anti-tank guns, whereupon the Tiger or Panther at the rear of the later inverted wedge could knock it out at long range.

And what of the Russian defence? Forewarned by the inevitability of the location of the German offensive, a foreknowledge that was at first confirmed and later fully amplified by the efforts of the 'Lucy' spy ring, the Russians had had over four months in which to prepare for the offensive. The main feature of this defence was its size: massive in terms of the men and matériel involved, and of the fixed defences around which the whole defence scheme was built. The first line of defences, built by troops and impressed civilian labour, consisted of five main trench lines over a depth of three miles. Carefully built into this system was a network of strongpoints and anti-tank positions, all interconnected and provided with underground bunkers as protection against the German artillery. Realising that the main weight of the German thrusts would lie with the armoured units, these anti-tank strongpoints (known to the Germans as Pakfronts) were the interlinked centrepieces of the Russian system. Each group of anti-tank guns was protected by dug-in tanks, field guns or machine gun nests, and amply protected by mines: Russian sources claim that the density of the minefields along the Soviet front was an average 2,400 anti-tank and 2,700 anti-personnel mines per mile of front, an extraordinarily high concentration.

A second line of defences, similar to the first, lay in wait for any German forces that might break through the first line and press on a further seven miles. A third line, also very strong, was 20 miles behind the second. The reserves were located about 40 miles behind the front, and they also dug their own massive system of defences. Should the Germans actually manage to break through all these lines, they would then encounter the theatre reserves, at first known as the Reserve Front and later as the Steppe Front, commanded by the redoubtable Colonel-General I.S. Konev. (The designation Front was used by the Russians for an army group.) This was located to the east of the salient, in a position where it could check any German advance

out of the salient, or before that move to aid either the northern or southern halves of the salient defences, but could not be drawn in or cut off too quickly. The location of the Steppe Front can only be described as masterly, and was the idea of General of the Army K. K. Rokossovsky, the commander of the Central Front.

The defences of the salient were manned by the troops of the Central Front already mentioned, from just south of Novosil to Korenevo (the northern half of the salient), and General of the Army N. F. Vatutin's Voronezh Front, from Korenevo to just north of Belgorod (the southern half of the salient). North of the salient, facing Orel, was Colonel-General M. M. Popov's Bryansk Front; south of it, facing Kharkov, was the South-West Front, commanded by Colonel-General R. Ya. Malinovsky.

The Steppe Front totalled five armies, including one tank army, as well as one tank, one mechanised and three cavalry corps; the Central Front had six armies, including one tank army, as well as two tank corps; and the Voronezh Front consisted of six armies, including one tank army, as well as one rifle (as the Russians designated infantry) and two tank corps.

Artillery support was provided for the two main Fronts by 13,000 guns, 6,000 anti-tank guns and 1,000 rocket-launchers, although some Soviet sources put the figure higher. Air support was given by the 2,500 aircraft (Soviet sources claim 1,900) of Lieutenant-General S. A. Krasovsky's 2nd Air Army and Lieutenant-General S. I. Rudenko's 16th Air Army. The question of Russian tank strength is a more difficult one. In his autobiography Zhukov claims that the Soviet forces had some 3,600 armoured fighting vehicles, but "The Battle of Kursk", edited by Major-General Ivan Parotkin, gives 1,800 to the Central Front, 1,700 to the Voronezh Front and 1,500 to the Steppe Front.

The Russian defensive plans were simple. Their forces would meet the German forces wherever the latter advanced and hold them as near the front as possible. On no account was a general retirement to be considered, and reserves were to be fed into the battle as proved necessary to hold and wear down the Germans in anticipation of the Russian counter-offensive on the flanks of the salient. As this developed, the forces in the salient were themselves to go over to the offensive against the Germans.

Unfortunately for the Germans, they were in considerable ignorance of the Russian dispositions: extensive aerial reconnaissance failed to pierce the Russian camouflage and find the enemy forces, and as the Russians held most of the high ground inside the salient they were safe from direct observation. The Germans, moreover, had to worry about the weather, and the date of any possible Allied landing in Europe. The Russians, on the other hand, had only to wait for the German onslaught. They knew the location and strength of the German forces, they knew where and when the German attacks would be coming; all that they did not know was the exact timing of the offensive's start.

A Soviet anti-aircraft machine gun crew dug in with their medium machine gun. The crew consists of a gunner, loader and commander who is adjusting the ring sight on the gun.

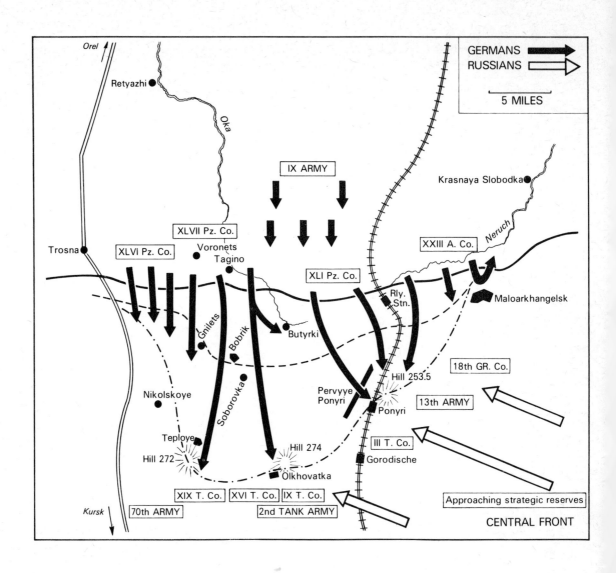

GERMANS
RUSSIANS

5 MILES

Orel

Retyazhi

Oka

IX ARMY

Krasnaya Slobodka

Neruch

XLVII Pz. Co.

Voronets

Tagino

XXIII A. Co.

Trosna

XLVI Pz. Co.

XLI Pz. Co.

Maloarkhangelsk

Rly. Stn.

Gnilets

Bobrik

Butyrki

Hill 253.5

18th GR. Co.

Nikolskoye

Soborovka

Pervyye Ponyri

Ponyri

13th ARMY

Teploye

Hill 274

III T. Co.

Gorodische

Hill 272

Olkhovatka

Approaching strategic reserves

Kursk

XIX T. Co.   XVI T. Co.   IX T. Co.

70th ARMY   2nd TANK ARMY

CENTRAL FRONT

14

3. Attack in the North

Forewarned of the German plans, the Russian Central Front started the Battle of Kursk in the north, with a sudden artillery bombardment of the German forming up positions and artillery lines early in the morning of July 5. The barrage started at 1.10 am and caused considerable damage, and some German commanders thought that the Russians were about to launch an offensive of their own – had they done so, they would have caught the Germans in an almost impossible position.

No Russian attack materialised, however, and right on schedule at 3.30 am the German barrage crashed out. Model had a heavier concentration of artillery than Manstein, and much was expected of this two-hour preliminary barrage. Such was the extent and strength of the Russian bunker complex that most of the front line troops were able to shelter in their bunkers to sit out the artillery storm and then emerge to face the first German infantry attack.

Model had decided to use his infantry in the first stage of the battle to clear the way for his armour through what were known to be very extensive Russian minefields. Indeed, during the period of postponement between April and early July, all Model's infantry formations had been rotated back to rear areas to practise on old Russian minefields. Severe though these had been, they were but pale imitations compared with the fields that they now encountered, and losses to the assault pioneers who led the way were very heavy. Whole parties up to battalion strength were pinned down and decimated by the excellently sited Russian strongpoints, most of which had survived the initial artillery bombardment. Nevertheless, the pioneers persevered, and gradually paths for the armour were cleared through these first Russian defences. Casualties had been so heavy, however, that commanders were forced to consider other means of achieving their ends. The 20th Panzer Division of XLVII Panzer Corps, whose way was to have been cleared by the routed 6th Division, was forced to send in its Ferdinand self-propelled tank-destroyers to pin down the Russian defences while the pioneers cleared the paths necessary for the rest of the division; in other places commanders used Goliath miniature tanks to save casualties. These were small tracked vehicles,

Key to Illustrations

Page 17 German Tiger tanks advancing towards the front prior to Operation Citadelle. They are part of a heavy tank company of the 1st Waffen S.S. Panzer Division the Leibstandarte Adolf Hitler. The lead tank has the crew's helmets slung on the turret and both vehicles have dust covers over their muzzle breaks. Though the Tiger's armour was not as well sloped as that of the Russian T34 or German Panther, it was thicker and the tank was armed with a powerful 8.8-cm KwK36 gun.

Page 18 Panzergrenadiers in their SdKfz 251 half tracks watch as a Russian village burns after an artillery bombardment. The SdKfz 251 carried the basic infantry squad of ten men with a driver and the commander. It had a maximum road speed of 33 mph and a range of about 186 miles cross-country. The vehicles shown carry 20 litre (5 gallon) petrol cans slung on the outer plates and coils of barbed wire. They are armed with a 7.62 MG34 machine gun with about 1,000 rounds of ammunition.

Page 19 A German machine gun and flame thrower team in action against a Russian strong point. The man operating the Kleif type man-pack flame thrower is covered by the machine gun crew with their MG34. The flame thrower had a range of between 15 and 25 yards at bursts of 12 seconds, it projected an oil based fuel. The MG34 had a rate of fire of between 800 and 900 rounds per minute and an effective range of 800 yards.

Page 20 A Panzerjager Elefant (Ferdinand) in action. This German anti-tank assault gun was armed with an 8.8-cm Pak 43/2 L/71 gun which only had a limited traverse. While this gun was very effective against all types of Russian armour, the Elefant did not carry a machine gun to defend itself against Russian infantry anti-tank teams armed with demolition charges. After the vehicles had been knocked out their considerable weight of 68 tons made them a major problem for the German recovery teams equipped with 18-ton half tracks.

Page 21 The commander of a Sturmgeschutz 40 Ausf (Mark) G spots his fire. The assault gun armed with a 7.5-cm gun and a machine gun is fitted with armoured skirts to cover the more vulnerable flanks against Russian anti-tank weapons. The assault gun has been coated with Zimmerit, a paste intended to proof the hull against magnetic anti-tank mines which could be placed by determined tank hunting teams. Also visible are spare tracks added as extra protection and spare road wheels stowed down the side of the vehicle by the armoured skirt.

Page 22 A Russian 76-mm anti-tank gun in action against German armour. The crew carry their personal weapons for close in defence against vehicle mounted German infantry. The 76-mm gun had a range of about 14,000 yards and a very high muzzle velocity. So short was the interval between the noise of the gun firing and the detonation of the shell the Germans coined the nick name "Ratsch-boom" or "Crash-bang" for the gun. It was the Russians' most effective anti-tank gun, though it was of simple design and characteristically rugged construction.

Page 23 A Panther Ausf D passes a burning Russian tank. The Panther is finished in basic sand coloured camouflage with green added. It is fitted with armoured skirts and spare road wheels have been added to the rear hull. The Panther, at Hitler's request, first saw action at Kursk and the early models were dogged with mechanical failures. However, when these had been rectified the tank with its well sloped armour and good speed became one of the most effective vehicles used by all the combatants during the Second World War.

Page 24 A Flakpanzer IV, quadruple 2-cm anti-aircraft guns on a PzKw IV chassis, in action against Russian ground attack aircraft. The gun had a rate of fire of 800 rounds per minute and was magazine fed with 20-round boxes. It was pedal operated and had a maximum horizontal range of 5,246 yards and a vertical range of 4,012 yards. In addition to four types of high explosive shell, the gun could also fire two types of armour piercing shell. The man in the foreground is using a range finder.

28

32

Page 25   A Russian Su-76 tank destroyer roars past a burning T34. The commander takes an in-cautious look over the top of his vehicle's armoured sides. The Su-76 had a crew of four men and was armed with one 76.2-mm gun with 62 rounds and some marks carried a 7.62-mm machine gun. The 140-hp engine had a maximum speed of 28 mph and a cross-country range of 185 miles. What it lacked in armour, its thickest was 25 mm, it made up for in speed and manoeuvrability and the powerful Model 42/3 anti-tank gun, made it a very effective tank killer.

Page 26   A PzKw IV, of the Waffen S.S. division Das Reich, opens fire during the fighting on the southern flank of the Kursk salient. The tank has been fitted with armoured skirts and extra track links. By the time of Operation Citadelle the PzKw IV was obsolescent, but up-armoured and up-gunned with a long 7.5-cm gun it could be used effectively with mixed Tiger and Panther units where it flushed out Russian tanks. Anti-tank guns were then knocked out at long range by the heavier guns of the newer German tanks.

Page 27   A Russian T34/76 B passes an abandoned disabled Porsche Elefant. The T34 had a road speed of 30 mph and a 500 horse power engine. Its broad tracks and Christie type suspension gave it a cross-country performance superior to many German types. Its 76.2-mm gun had rudimentary sights, but Russian tank commanders compensated for these deficiencies by closing with their enemy so that accurate sights were not necessary. With a radius of action of 280 miles the T34 spear-headed the Russian drive westwards following Kursk.

Page 28   A Pak 38 5-cm anti-tank gun in action. The Pak 38 could penetrate 2.5 mm of vertical armour at 1,200 yards and could fire high explosive as well as armour piercing ammunition. The gun crew were protected by an armoured shield which consisted of two sheets of 4 mm armour with a one inch space between the plates. They are armed with the standard Mauser 98K rifle and a 9-mm pistol, probably a Walther P 38.

Page 29   Two ground attack Henschel Hs 129 B-1 fighters fly low over the steppe after attacking a column of Russian tanks. The Henschel 129 was armed with two 7.9-mm machine guns and two 20-mm cannon and could carry a 30-mm cannon under the fuselage with 30 rounds of armour piercing ammunition. Heavily armoured the Henschel had a maximum speed of 253 mph at 12,500 feet and a range of 348 miles. In concert with the Stuka (Ju 87) it was a deadly weapon against armour and infantry.

Page 30   With a DPM light machine gunner at the front, a party of Russian assault pioneers clear a German held trench. They are armed with hand grenades, the standard Mosin Nagant 7.62-mm rifle and the PPSH sub-machine gun. The man on the left has an entrenching tool slung from his belt, and all the soldiers carry greatcoats or blankets slung bandolier fashion. The DPM machine gun had a 47-round pan magazine on top of the gun which gave it a rate of fire of 600 rounds per minute.

Page 31   An Ilushin I 1-2m3 Shturmovik painted with the slogan "Avenger" climbs above a column of German tanks and trucks. The Shturmovik had a maximum speed of 251 mph and a range of 375 miles. It could carry a wide range of under wing ordnance including a DAG grenade launcher, eight RS 82 or RS 132 rockets, 1,321 lb bomb load, or 200 PTAB 2, 5-1, 5 anti-tank bombs, besides its standard armament of two N-37 or P-37 anti-tank cannon, two Shkas 7.62-mm machine guns and one BS 12.7-mm machine gun.

Page 32   A Klimenti Voroshilov KV 1C heavy tank roars past its victim, a German 10.5-cm Wespe light howitzer. The KV 1 armed with a 76.2-mm gun and three machine guns had a maximum speed of 26 mph. Bigger and heavier than the T34 it carried the same gun, but a larger stock of ammunition, 111 rounds as against 77. The Degtyarev machine gun in the rear of the turret was protection against infantry armed with short range anti-tank weapons or demolition charges.

fitted with a heavy explosive charge and remotely controlled through wires, which could be steered onto their targets and there detonated with considerable effect.

Russian sources claim considerable numbers of tanks knocked out in the first two days of the attack, but during this period only the 20th Panzer Division and some companies of Ferdinand guns had been committed. Nevertheless, during the first day steady, although costly, progress was made by the 258th, 7th, 31st, 20th Panzer, 6th, 292nd, 86th, 78th and 216th Divisions against the 280th Rifle, 132nd Rifle, 15th Rifle, 81st Rifle, 294th Rifle and 254th Rifle Divisions of the 70th Army (Lieutenant-General I. V. Galinin), 2nd Tank Army (Lieutenant-General A. G. Rodin) and 13th Army (Lieutenant-General N. P. Pukhov). The major German reverses of the day had been the initial repulse of the 6th Division already mentioned, and the continued failure of the 383rd Division to take the key town of Maloarchangelsk on the extreme left of the German assault area. The town was very stoutly defended by the 254th and 148th Rifle Divisions.

By the evening of July 5, the Germans had advanced on a 30-mile front to a maximum depth of six miles, the furthest progress being made in the centre, in the area of the villages of Gnilets, Bobrik and Butyrki. The Russians had managed to hold on to the first, but the other two had fallen to the Germans. Although they had been pushed back on a wide front, the Russians had learned some lessons that were to prove invaluable to them. Principal amongst these was the vulnerability of the monstrous 72-ton Ferdinand, which lacked a defensive machine gun: if its supporting infantry could be pinned down by machine gun fire, a Russian could approach and destroy a Ferdinand by placing a charge against the undefended and more thinly armoured sides or rear of the vehicle. Some commanders were reduced to desperate measures in efforts to protect their vehicles from such attacks, including the firing of a hand-held machine gun down the barrel of the 8.8-cm gun, which was, in any event, capable of only a limited traverse.

Model was not satisfied with the day's progress, and on the 6th decided to throw in major elements of his Panzer forces, which he had hoped to reserve for the drive on Kursk after the infantry had broken through the Russian defences. First to be used were the 2nd Panzer, 9th Panzer and 18th Panzer Divisions. These Model committed in the central sector of the front in an effort to take the dominating heights of Hills 272, just south of Teploye, 274, just north of Olkhovatka, and 253.5, just east of Ponyri. If these hills could be taken, the Germans would be in possession of the ridge that constituted the major obstacle between themselves and Kursk. Indeed, from the top of the ridge, Kursk could be seen 40 miles away and 400 feet below. Moreover, with this ridge in his possession, Model would be able to take on the Russian reserves that were beginning to arrive in great numbers on terrain unfavourable to the latter. The Russians, too, had realised this, and Rokossovsky was reinforcing his line with all the armour he could muster. Two tank corps arrived during the night of July 6-7 and launched a counter-attack which soon broke down on the Russians' own minefields, which had been strengthened by the Germans once they had passed through them. By the 9th the ridge was defended by the XIX Tank, XVI Tank, IX Tank, III Tank and XVIII Guards Rifle Corps; and between July 7 and 9 there raged over the area between Teploye and Ponyri armoured battles exceeded in scope only by those at Prokhorovka in the southern half of the salient.

Model's intention had been to ward off the inevitable approach of Russian armoured reinforcements from the east by a deep thrust by XXIII Corps through Maloarchangelsk to the south. The corps would then form a front to the south-east to prevent the arrival of Rokossovsky's reserves. But with the failure of the corps to penetrate through Maloarchangelsk, there was no way of halting the arrival of fresh Russian forces – and the Germans had few reserves, all of them short of armour.

The combination of new forces, especially the tank corps, and the existing fine network of anti-tank strongpoints made the German task all but impossible. Yet the Panzer divisions and the independent 505th Tiger Tank Battalion, together with their attached assault pioneers, infantry and supporting arms, fought on with great courage against terrible opposition. Moreover, the Germans were not only encountering large quantities of Russian troops, but also men of high fighting abilities. The Russians had now learned from their mistakes of the previous two years and had trained their men well – no longer did the thought of German armour terrify the Russian infantry into headlong flight; instead they stood and fought with great tenacity. If they were forced back they immediately launched a counter-attack to retake their positions – Teploye was lost and retaken three times, and Paul Carell aptly describes the fighting for Ponyri as the 'Stalingrad of the Kursk salient'.

The tank battles were also savage affairs, with upwards of 2,000 armoured fighting vehicles involved in a small area. This was a decided disadvantage to the Germans, whose superior guns and gunnery could have been used to better advantage at longer range. The Russians, however, using their T-34s' and KV-1s' greater manoeuvrability and speed, kept the range as short as possible, where their lack of sophisticated fire-control equipment was no hindrance, and where their guns could cause as much damage to the new German tanks as could the Germans to the Russians.

The battle ebbed and flowed, but gradually the Germans pushed forward against ever strengthening Russian defences despite their own considerable casualties. But the Germans' rate of advance was terribly slow, and slowed further every hour as more Russian forces made their appearance on the battlefield. No matter how many anti-tank strongpoints were overrun by the German tanks, there always seemed to be another behind it. The tanks had to go it alone, as no infantry could survive in an area so dominated by ground-attack aircraft, machine gun nests, anti-tank strongpoints and the ever-present plunging fire of the Russian heavy artillery.

On July 8 Model committed his last fully armoured division, the 4th Panzer. Carell gives a graphic description of its battle on that day, a description that exemplifies the sort of action a Panzer division had to fight during the struggle for the Kursk salient. The division was commanded by Lieutenant-General D. von Saucken, and took over from the 20th Panzer and 2nd Panzer Divisions the task of pushing on from Gnilets to Teploye and the essential Hill 272.

Supported by Ju 87 dive-bombers to suppress the Russian artillery and Henschel Hs 129 ground-attack aircraft to attack troop concentrations and armour, the division moved up, with the remnants of the 20th and 2nd Panzer Divisions, against the defences of Teploye. These had been built up considerably by Rokossovsky, as he realised that this was one of the decisive points on the front: two rifle divisions, one artillery division, one mechanised rifle brigade and two tank brigades.

Losing 100 men in the process, the 2nd Battalion of the 33rd Panzergrenadier Regiment drove forward through an almost solid wall of artillery and machine gun fire to force the Russian defenders out of the village. But beyond the village lay the last line of hills before the ground sloped away to Kursk, and the Russians fell back to this to regroup. Saucken wished to give the Russians no time to organise a defence of the hill line or to retake the village, and ordered his men to press forward with all speed.

The division's spearhead was now formed by the 3rd and 35th Panzer Regiments, with accompanying infantry and Panzergrenadiers in armoured half-tracks. Air support was called in again, and the Germans plunged forward. But they were faced by an experienced and highly skilled opponent in the form of the 3rd Anti-Tank Artillery Brigade. This was also given additional firepower by numerous T-34 tanks that had been dug into the hillside. Poised to take the Germans in flank as they advanced up the hill were also numerous infantrymen armed with anti-tank rifles, which in the hands of steady men were quite efficient against older tanks.

The Germans advanced as quickly as they could through a rain of Russian shells to close with the enemy, where artillery support could not be called for by the Russians. But the artillery fire was too much for the infantry, who had to take cover, leaving the tanks to push on alone.

Displaying remarkable courage, the Russians let the German armour approach to the point-blank range of 400 metres before opening fire. At ranges as close as this even the Tigers' massive frontal armour was no protection against anti-tank shells, and German losses were heavy. Yet the survivors drove on, and overran the Russian positions, wreaking terrible destruction with their guns and treads. Once the tanks were amongst the Russian positions, the Panzergrenadiers were able to charge forward from where they had taken cover and clear the hilltop.

Exhausted by their efforts, however, the Germans were almost immediately driven back from the top by a determined Russian counter-attack. The battle for Hill 272 continued for another two days, during which the Germans twice again took the top, and were twice driven back. By the beginning of the third attack, the 33rd Panzergrenadier Regiment had been shattered. The only officer left in the 2nd Battalion, Captain Diesener, led the last attack with all that was left of the battalion, took the hill and was driven back for the last time.

The story was much the same during the battle for Hill 274 at Olkhovatka, where the 6th Division managed to take only the lower slopes of the hill, leaving the Russians in control of the dominating top.

The last strategically vital hilltop was that of Hill 253.5, near Ponyri. The Russians held on grimly against the last efforts of the 18th Panzer and 9th Panzer Divisions, supported by the 292nd and 86th Divisions. The Germans managed to take the smaller hills on each side of Hill 253.5, but again failed to dislodge the Russians, whose effort was headed by the sterling defence and constant counter-attacks of the 1032nd Rifle Regiment.

On July 11 Model threw in his last armoured force, the 10th Panzergrenadier Division, to take over from the 292nd Division, which had been all but destroyed. The Russians, realising that the hour of decision had arrived, also threw in further forces, and counter-attacked on the morning that the 10th Panzergrenadiers moved into their positions. This division had the high artillery complement of seven battalions of guns, a regiment of Nebelwerfer rocket launchers, a battalion of heavy mortars and a battalion of assault guns. This quantity of firepower was just sufficient to check the Russian counter-attack on the 11th. A further three counter-attacks on Ponyri were beaten off on the 12th. Over the next few days the Russians attacked time and time again, only to be checked by the artillery of Lieutenant-General A. Schmidt's 10th Panzergrenadier Division. But although they failed to retake Ponyri, the Russians had achieved their objectives: they had halted the attempts of Model's 9th Army to advance south to Kursk. Indeed, having advanced five miles on the first day of their offensive, in the next seven days the Germans pushed on only another six miles before being halted before the ridge that would have afforded them a downhill run to Kursk.

Rokossovsky had played his cards with consummate skill. Not afraid to suffer very heavy casualties, he had fed in massive reinforcements as and when needed, and had not let himself be drawn into a battle on unfavourable terms. But had the left wing of Model's effort contained some armour, enabling it to break through at Maloarchangelsk and prevent Russian reinforcements reaching the main battlefield, the story might (but only might) have been different. As it was, the Germans had exhausted both men and matériel, and were ripe for the massive Russian counter-offensive that was about to descend on them in a matter of days. The Germans had gambled on being able to achieve a strategic breakthrough swiftly, as in the early days of the war. But the Russians had not collapsed and so the Germans were forced to fight a battle of attrition against an enemy they stood virtually no chance of beating.

4. Attack in the South

In the south, Manstein's forces attacked at 3.00 pm on July 4, 12 hours before the start of Model's half of the German pincer in the north. The aim of this early start was to secure the line of hills immediately in front of the German front line, to facilitate the beginning of the main offensive on the next day.

Preceded by a heavy carpet bombing of the main assault area and a short artillery bombardment, the main attack was launched by XLVIII Panzer Corps of Hoth's 4th Panzerarmee on the central sector of the front. Although the Russians were aware that a major offensive was about to break, Lieutenant-General I. M. Chistyakov's 6th Guards Army, defending this sector of the front, was taken unaware by the tactically unorthodox timing of Hoth's attack, and the 3rd Panzer, 'Grossdeutschland' Panzergrenadier and 11th Panzer Divisions swept all before them. In three hours the German armoured formations had moved up some three miles, taking the key villages of Gertsovka and Butovo before the Russians could recover from their surprise, and securing the line of hills that was their objective. (Despite its Panzergrenadier designation,

the 'Grossdeutschland' Division was the strongest armoured formation used in the offensive, with some 180 tanks.)

On the left of XLVIII Panzer Corps, LII Corps had also attacked, but only to pin the Russian defenders in the area and to secure observation posts for the main offensive. On the right of XLVIII Panzer Corps, II SS Panzer Corps also launched subsidiary attacks during the night to win their own observation posts for the next day's offensive. Further German preparations, however, were disrupted by two factors. At 10.30 pm the Russians fired a massive artillery shoot to keep the Germans off balance, and during the night there was a torrential rainstorm. This was particularly unfortunate for the Germans, as it turned the sandy soil of the region into a quagmire, making the going poor for the tanks and other armoured vehicles.

Knowing that the German intention was to strike straight towards Kursk through Oboyan, the Russians had deployed their powerful armoured reserves in great depth along the expected German route. Chief of these reserve forces was the 1st Tank

Army, commanded by Lieutenant-General M. Y. Katukov, with the VI Tank, XXXI Tank, V Guards Tank and III Mechanised Corps. The 69th Army (Lieutenant-General V. D. Kryuchenkin) was also well placed south of Prokhorovka to come to the aid of the 6th Guards and 1st Tank Armies. Further to the east again, one of Konev's most powerful formations, the 5th Guards Tank Army (Lieutenant-General P. A. Rotmistrov) was ready to move out to support Vatutin's armies in case of need.

Aerial reconnaissance had revealed the location of many of these elements to Hoth, who also disliked the OKH instructions that he was to strike towards Kursk by the direct (and therefore most obvious) route. He realised that his advance would inevitably pull forward the Russian reserves to meet him at Oboyan, and that these reserves would have to move across the neck of land between the Donets and Psel rivers which had Prokhorovka at its centre. Hoth therefore decided to interpret his orders to allow him to attack first due north, but then swing to the north-east, where he could meet the Russian reinforcements near Prokhorovka, defeat them and then resume his advance to Kursk against lighter resistance. The swing to the north-east would also help the forces of Operational Group 'Kempf' on the right wing of the 4th Panzerarmee to keep up after its crossing of the Donets south of Belgorod and subsequent wheel to the north to cover the 4th Panzerarmee's right flank. As Hoth's tactical decision was made without the knowledge of OKH, there was no way that the 'Lucy' ring could get to know of it, and therefore no way that the Russians could alter their tactical dispositions before the event to counter the threat. Thus Hoth's decision was to have very important long-term results.

The main phase of the southern assault began at 3.30 am on July 5 with a massive artillery bombardment, followed by the advance of the land forces involved at 5.00 am. But unlike Model's offensive in the north, Manstein's was spearheaded by the armour, not by the infantry, as Manstein considered that his infantry resources were too slender to squander in opening the way for the armour against heavy Russian resistance. They

would be needed for more important tasks later. Therefore the tanks set off in the lead, although not without considerable trouble. Firstly, the new tank types (Tiger and Panther) were still plagued by teething troubles, and secondly, many of the Panzer battalions found themselves trying to cross hitherto unsuspected Russian anti-tank minefields. The first stage of the offensive was therefore slow and costly. Losses on the minefields amongst the Panthers of Lieutenant-Colonel von Lauchert's Panther brigade led to the failure of the first German assault on the village of Butovo itself, which had been reached the night before. But by 7.30 am all the German first objectives had been reached, and the men and tanks of XLVIII Panzer Corps pressed on.

By the end of the day's fighting the 3rd Panzer Division, on the corps' left wing, had pushed on to Krasnyy Pochinok, taking the important Hill 220 and the village of Korovino after a stiff fight in the process. In the centre the 'Grossdeutschland' Division finally managed to take Cherkasskoye against strenuous Russian resistance with the aid of elements of the 11th Panzer Division, Knobelsdorff's right-wing armoured formation, which had also probed some 10 miles up the road to Oboyan.

Better progress was made by Hausser's II SS Panzer Corps on XLVIII Panzer Corps' right. It was in this sector that Chistyakov expected the Germans to make their main effort, and he was not disappointed – the corps facing his left wing was the same formation that had retaken Kharkov in Manstein's remarkable counter-offensive in the spring. The divisions of the SS Panzer Corps were three élite units: the 1st SS Panzer Division 'Leibstandarte Adolf Hitler', the 2nd SS Panzer Division 'Das Reich' and the 3rd SS Panzer Division 'Totenkopf', with much of the best new matériel and reinforcements. The corps' armoured strength was some 300 tanks, including a large proportion of Tigers, and 120 assault guns. The Russian front line defence lay in the hands of only two infantry divisions, the 52nd Guards Rifle and 375th Rifle Divisions, but both were of a high quality, and defence in depth was provided by the divisions of Katukov's 1st Tank Army.

The Germans expected much of the efforts of

VIII Fliegerkorps, and indeed some 2,400 sorties were flown with considerable success against Russian rear-area concentrations. But the day had almost proved a disaster for the Germans. Knowing the Fliegerkorps' plans, the Russians themselves launched a pre-emptive strike on the German airfields, intending to catch the German aircraft forming up at dawn and so destroy them on the ground. The Russians very nearly succeeded, and might well have done so had not a few examples of Freya ground-to-air radar been recently installed. With this apparatus the Germans detected the approach of the Russian bombing force in just enough time to scramble their fighters to intercept. The Russian bombers were savagely mauled, and the raid failed, leaving the Germans to launch their own strike against their Russian targets.

At the appointed hour the German Panzer

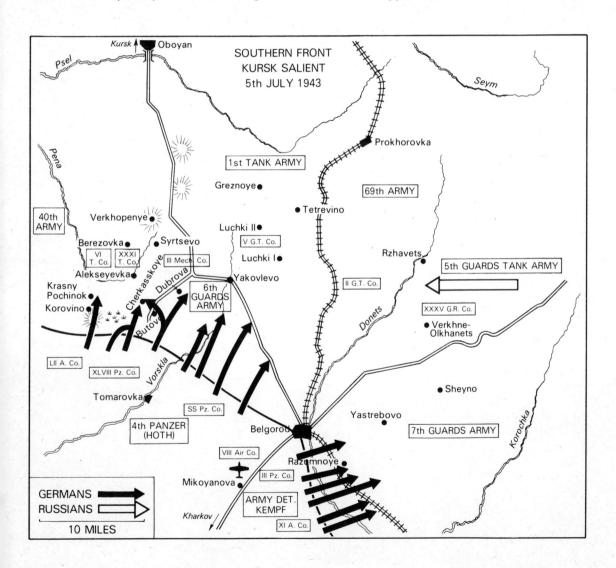

SOUTHERN FRONT
KURSK SALIENT
5th JULY 1943

Kursk ↑ Oboyan
Psel
Seym
Prokhorovka
1st TANK ARMY
Greznoye
69th ARMY
Pena
Tetrevino
40th ARMY
Verkhopenye
Luchki II
V G.T. Co.
Berezovka
Syrtsevo
Luchki I
Rzhavets
VI T. Co.
XXXI T. Co.
III Mech. Co.
5th GUARDS TANK ARMY
Alekseyevka
Cherkasskoye
Dubrova
Yakovlevo
II G.T. Co.
Krasny Pochinok
6th GUARDS ARMY
XXXV G.R. Co.
Korovino
Butovo
Verkhne-Olkhanets
Donets
LII A. Co.
Vorskla
XLVIII Pz. Co.
Sheyno
Tomarovka
SS Pz. Co.
Yastrebovo
4th PANZER (HOTH)
Belgorod
7th GUARDS ARMY
Korochka
VIII Air Co.
Razumnoye
Mikoyanova
III Pz. Co.
GERMANS
RUSSIANS
ARMY DET. KEMPF
Kharkov
10 MILES
XI A. Co.

39

divisions crashed forward, and at first made good general progress except on the front of the 'Leibstandarte' Division, where there was extremely stubborn Russian resistance. But then the Germans played their trump card: Ju 87 dive-bombers used a new type of fragmentation bomb with devastating effect on the Russian artillery positions, which as usual were the linch-pins of the Soviet defence, and Henschel 129 ground-attack aircraft with a 2-cm cannon mounted under the fuselage savaged the Russian rear-area armour concentrations, preventing them from being moved up. These two new weapons so unseamed the Russian defence that the German advance picked up momentum so rapidly that Chistyakov himself was nearly captured at his headquarters. By the end of the day the 'Leibstandarte', supported on its left by the 167th Division, had moved some 10 miles up along the course of the Vorskla river, whilst on its right the 'Das Reich' and 'Totenkopf' Divisions had advanced an average of 12 miles each to reach the Belgorod-Oboyan road after breaking through the 52nd Guards Rifle Division's defences. The Germans were through the first line of Russian fixed defences.

The position at the end of the first day of Zitadelle was worse in the sector of Operational Group 'Kempf', whose fast advance was vital to protect the 4th Panzerarmee's right flank from the reserves that were sure to be called in from the Steppe Front as the German advance gathered pace. Just south of Belgorod, III Panzer Corps' divisions (168th, 6th Panzer, 19th Panzer and 7th Panzer) had established themselves in a bridgehead seven miles across and five miles deep on the east bank of the Donets; to its south the 106th and 320th Divisions had established a similar but slightly smaller bridgehead.

The German progress had been significant, but none of the three advances was as great as was called for in the schedule – and speed was all-important to the German overall plan. Moreover, Russian resistance had been considerably more determined and efficient than had been anticipated. Admittedly the waterlogged ground had slowed down the German advance after the main forces had broken through the Russian defences, but nonetheless the Russians had pulled back in good order, giving the Germans none of the vast masses of captured men and matériel they were used to. From the German point of view the picture was a disturbing one – and their forces had yet to meet the second Russian defence line, just as formidable as the first one.

On July 6 the Germans again advanced against strengthening Russian resistance as the formations of the 1st Tank Army moved up in support of the 6th Guards Army. A notable realisation of the day was the inability of VIII Fliegerkorps to fly adequate missions in support of both XLVIII Panzer and II SS Panzer Corps and give some measure of aid to III Panzer Corps. Nevertheless, the reinforced Russian anti-tank units of the second defence line were decimated by the German fragmentation bombs. In a further effort to strengthen their anti-tank capabilities, the Russians decided to dig in a large number of their tanks, even though this would lose them all the mobility that had proved so useful in the past. There was considerable argument about this at the time, and it was to have important consequences for tank availability during the tank battles at Prokhorovka.

At last on July 7 there was a definite possibility of a German breakthrough. This would have given the Germans the room for manoeuvre they so desperately needed to crush the numerically stronger Russian forces, and did in fact cause a considerable amount of anxiety in the Russian high command. On the left of the attack, XLVIII Panzer Corps' 'Grossdeutschland' and 11th Panzer Divisions made steady progress towards Oboyan, despite furious counter-attacks by VI Tank Corps, whilst to their right II SS Panzer Corps' 'Leibstandarte' and 'Totenkopf' Divisions moved north and then north-west to meet the advanced units of XLVIII Panzer Corps, and the 'Das Reich' Division pushed forward on Prokhorovka against the determined resistance of II Guards Tank and II Tank Corps.

More importantly, south of Belgorod, Breith switched his 6th Panzer Division from his left to his right wing where, in conjunction with the 7th Panzer Division, it began to make rapid progress northwards to cover Hauser's right wing. III Panzer Corps was thus moving across the front held by

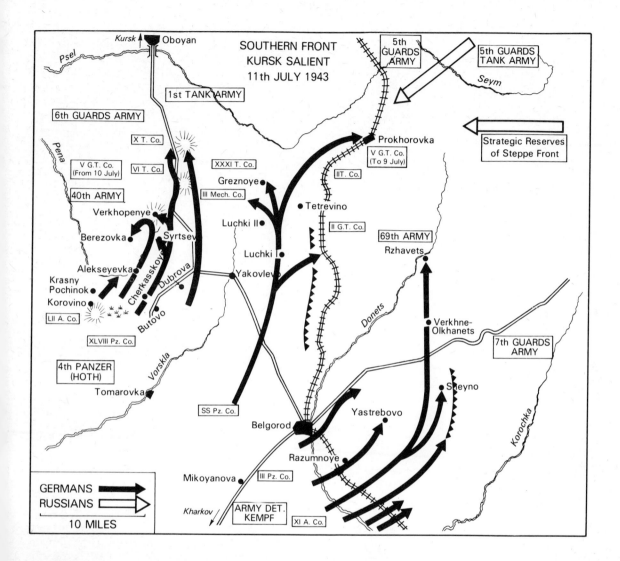

Psel
Kursk ↑ Oboyan

SOUTHERN FRONT
KURSK SALIENT
11th JULY 1943

5th
GUARDS
ARMY

5th GUARDS
TANK ARMY

Seym

1st TANK ARMY

6th GUARDS ARMY

Strategic Reserves
of Steppe Front

Pena

X T. Co.

V G.T. Co.
(From 10 July)

VI T. Co.

40th ARMY

XXXI T. Co.

III Mech. Co.

Greznoye

V G.T. Co.
(To 9 July)

Prokhorovka

IIT. Co.

Verkhopenye

Berezovka

Syrtsev

Alekseyevka

Krasny
Pochinok

Korovino

Cherkasskoye

Dubrova

Butovo

LII A. Co.

XLVIII Pz. Co.

Luchki II

Tetrevino

II G.T. Co.

Luchki

Yakovlevo

69th ARMY

Rzhavets

Donets

Verkhne-
Olkhanets

7th GUARDS
ARMY

4th PANZER
(HOTH)

Tomarovka

Vorskla

SS Pz. Co.

Belgorod

Yastrebovo

Sheyno

Korochka

Razumnoye

Mikoyanova

III Pz. Co.

Kharkov

ARMY DET.
KEMPF

XI A. Co.

GERMANS
RUSSIANS

10 MILES

Lieutenant-General M. S. Shumilov's 7th Guards Army. The Russian commander in the area, Vatutin, had to take the dangerous step of taking all their artillery from the unengaged 38th Army (Lieutenant-General N. Y. Chisibov) and 40th Army (Lieutenant-General K. S. Moskalenko) in the south-west corner of the salient to bolster the 7th Guards Army's defences. The two armies also had to give up some other forces to provide a covering defence for Oboyan. Breith's advance was helped after July 9 by the pinning attacks launched on Shumilov's left wing by the marching infantry of XI Corps.

But by July 9 XLVIII Panzer Corps had been halted, still 15 miles from Oboyan and 90 miles from the most southerly of Model's forces. II SS Panzer Corps' advance was also slowing, leaving III Panzer Corps as the fastest moving German formation of the day. Nonetheless, the corps was advancing on its own, for it was moving up a corridor bounded on the west by the 81st Guards Rifle, 375th Rifle and 51st Guards Rifle Divisions (which with II Guards Tank Corps also provided a cordon against any eastern advance by II SS Panzer Corps), and on the east by the 73rd Guards Rifle, 94th Guards Rifle and 305th Rifle Divisions of the 7th Guards Army.

This would have been the ideal moment for Vatutin to launch a major counter-attack against XLVIII Panzer and II SS Panzer Corps, but as noted above a large proportion of his armoured forces had been dug in in defensive positions, and could not therefore be extricated in time. The Stavka now allotted Rotmistrov's 5th Guards Tank Army and Lieutenant-General A. S. Zhadov's 5th Guards Army, both from the Steppe Front to the Voronezh Front as the necessary counter-attack force. The two armies set off from their concentration areas 200 miles to the east by forced marches.

Rotmistrov's armoured forces, consisting of four tank and one mechanised corps, reached Prokhorovka on the 12th. But where was III Panzer Corps? Anticipating that the Russians would react just as they had, Hoth had planned to have Breith's corps across the neck of land at Prokhorovka to block off the Russian reinforcements. Yet Breith had not arrived, and the danger to Hausser's right or southern flank had been all too clearly revealed on the 8th when only a major Luftwaffe ground-attack effort had saved the unsuspecting 'Das Reich' Division from being taken in flank by II Guards Tank Corps.

Breith's corps had been held up by sterling Russian resistance, and so II SS Panzer Corps was left to fight the fresh 5th Guards Tank Army on its own. XLVIII Panzer Corps could offer little help as it was fully engaged against the heavily battered but still cohesive 6th Guards and 1st Tank Armies.

The tank battle at Prokhorovka, which started on July 12 and continued until the German offensive was called off, was the largest single tank action in history: the Russians started with some 850 armoured fighting vehicles, and the Germans with about 600. Both sides were to be considerably reinforced during the battle, so the total number of AFVs involved was certainly well over 2,000.

The Russians started the battle in the morning of the 12th with a massive bombing raid, and then immediately plunged into battle with their armoured forces. It was a desperate and titanic struggle, fought over steep hills covered in orchards and cut up by narrow streams – terrain, in fact, in which the Germans could not use the better long-range performance of their tank guns to full advantage, but in which the Russians could site their SU-76, 85, 122 and 152 tank-destroyers with excellent results.

For hours the outcome of the battle was in doubt, the freshness of the Russian forces balancing the superior skills and matériel of Hausser's corps. The commander of the 5th Guards Tank Army, Rotmistrov, has given a good account of the battle:

'Our tanks advanced across the steppe in small groups, using copses and hedges as cover. Initial staccato gunfire soon merged into a great sustained roar. The Russian tanks met the German advanced formations flat out and pushed through the German armoured screen. At the close ranges that resulted, T-34s knocked out Tigers as the latters' powerful guns and massive armour no longer conferred any advantage. Both sides' tanks were mixed up together, and there was no opportunity, either in time or space, to disengage and reform in battle order, or to fight in battle formation. So short was the range that our shells pierced not only the side but also the frontal armour of the German tanks. At ranges so short armour offered no protection, and gun barrel length conferred no advantage. When a tank was hit, frequently its turret was blown off and tossed through the air for dozens of yards. At the same time, over the battlefield furious air fighting built up, with both Russian and German airmen trying to help their own sides. Prokhorovka seemed to be permanently in the shadow of bomber, ground-attack and fighter aircraft, and one dogfight seemed to follow another without respite. In no time the sky seemed to be palled by the smoke of the various wrecks. The earth was black and scorched with tanks burning like torches.

'The 2nd Battalion of the 181st Tank Brigade

of XVIII Tank Corps, attacking down the left-hand bank of the Psel river, ran into a group of German Tigers, which opened up on the Russian tanks from a stationary position. Realising the long-range capabilities of the German guns, the Russian tanks tried to close quickly to obviate this advantage. Captain P. A. Skripkin, the battalion's commander, ordered his other tanks to follow him. His first shell penetrated a Tiger's side armour, but immediately another Tiger opened fire on Skripkin's T-34. The first shell came in through the side, and the second wounded Skripkin himself. The driver and the wireless operator dragged their commander out of the tank and hauled him into the shelter of a shell crater. A Tiger was bearing right down on them, so Aleksandr Nikolaiev, the driver, clambered back into his damaged and smouldering

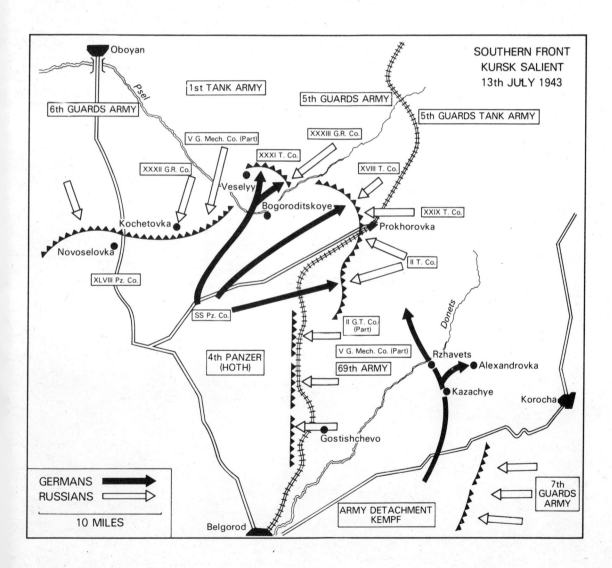

SOUTHERN FRONT
KURSK SALIENT
13th JULY 1943

Oboyan

1st TANK ARMY

5th GUARDS ARMY

5th GUARDS TANK ARMY

6th GUARDS ARMY

Psel

V G. Mech. Co. (Part)

XXXIII G.R. Co.

XXXII G.R. Co.

XXXI T. Co.

XVIII T. Co.

Veselyy

Bogoroditskoye

XXIX T. Co.

Kochetovka

Prokhorovka

Novoselovka

II T. Co.

XLVIII Pz. Co.

Donets

SS Pz. Co.

II G.T. Co. (Part)

4th PANZER (HOTH)

V G. Mech. Co. (Part)

Rzhavets

Alexandrovka

69th ARMY

Kazachye

Korocha

Gostishchevo

GERMANS

RUSSIANS

10 MILES

7th GUARDS ARMY

Belgorod

ARMY DETACHMENT KEMPF

43

tank, started up and charged towards the German tank. The T-34 hurtled across the ground like a fireball; the Tiger halted, but it was too late. The blazing T-34 hit the German tank at full speed, and the explosion made the very ground shake.'

Whilst the furious struggle was being waged at Prokhorovka, the events that were to decide the tactical outcome of the battle were being decided further to the south, where Breith's III Panzer Corps was racing up to meet II SS Panzer Corps and take the 6th Guards Tank Army in flank. III Corps was held up at Rzhavets, on the Donets river

12 miles south of Prokhorovka. Here determined Russian resistance had halted the 6th Panzer Division. But on the night of July 12-13 the Germans took Rzhavets by a coup de main, a captured T-34 leading a column of German armour into the town and then taking it, allowing the Germans to push on to Prokhorovka. The Russian left flank was completely exposed, and the 6th Panzer, 7th Panzer and 19th Panzer Divisions were free to drive up into Rotmistrov's bare flank. Nothing could stop the Germans from winning a great victory – or so they thought. But far away events were occurring that were to shatter the German dream of a great success at Kursk.

Three Klimenti Voroshilov KV1 tanks on the move in the dust of the Russian steppe.

5. The End of the Battle

On July 13 Field-Marshals von Kluge and von Manstein, commanders of Army Groups 'Centre' and 'South' respectively, were summoned to a meeting with Hitler at the latter's headquarters at Rastenburg in East Prussia. The two Eastern Front commanders flew in, and were promptly informed by the Führer that Operation 'Zitadelle' was to be called off. Hitler's reasoning for this decision was simple: three days earlier, on July 10, strong forces had been landed in Sicily by the Western Allies. Italian resistance had not been worthy of the name, and there was now every indication that Italy was about to pull out of the war, leaving the Germans in an almost untenable position in the Mediterranean. Hitler expected further Allied landings on the Italian mainland or in the Balkans at any time, and therefore Zitadelle must be called off and the armoured forces involved shipped to the Mediterranean to check any Allied landings. Hitler entirely ignored the logistical fact that it would take months to move so many men and all their equipment to the Mediterranean.

Kluge agreed with Hitler that Zitadelle should be called off, but for different reasons. His 9th Army was making no progress in the great battle around Olkhovatka in the northern half of the salient, and would not even be able to renew its offensive, and Kluge needed to move Model's armoured forces to reinforce Colonel-General R. Schmidt's 2nd Panzerarmee. This army had been holding the sector of the German salient around Orel not involved in the Battle of Kursk, and had on the previous day, July 12, been heavily attacked by the forces of Popov's Bryansk Front. Although the Germans as yet did not know it, this was the first stage of the great Russian summer offensive into which the German plans for the Kursk battle had been incorporated. Kluge therefore intended to call off Model's operations between Teploye and Olkhovatka in favour of a determined resistance to the Russian thrusts that were now threatening Orel, and with it the security of the whole German salient.

Manstein disagreed with Hitler's decision to call off the whole offensive. Even if Kluge had to halt Model in favour of checking Popov's advances, he argued, there was every reason to persevere with the southern half of the offensive: clearly the territorial objectives of the initial plan would have to be given up, but there still remained the opportunity of inflicting a severe defeat to the Russians. Manstein argued that the Russians had committed all their reserves (in fact one rifle and two tank corps of the Central Front had not yet been committed), and that II SS Panzer and III Panzer Corps could wipe out a sizable Russian force south of Prokhorovka. For in the south the final arrival of III Panzer Corps from Rzhavets had put the Soviet counter-attack in a very dangerous position. The 69th Army, and with it II Tank and II Guards Tank Corps, were all but encircled, and the Germans were close to achieving a decisive tactical victory.

Hitler agreed with both his commanders: Kluge

was allowed to halt Model, but Manstein was allowed to order Hoth to press on with his battle as fast as he could. On the 17th, however, just as victory came in sight, Hitler ordered Manstein to call off his half of the offensive, and prepare II SS Panzer Corps for transfer to Italy. At the same time he was to give two Panzer divisions to Kluge to try to check the Russian advance in the north.

And so ended the German effort to eliminate the Kursk salient, and with it the last strategical initiative Germany was to be allowed in the East. The whole offensive had been poorly conceived and then let down by the timidity on the part of the German high command, especially Hitler himself, which led to postponement after postponement. Albert Seaton sums it up well in his 'The Russo-German War 1941-1945': 'Up to 1943 the Germans usually succeeded tactically but failed strategically. At Kursk

A Soviet anti-tank rifle crew in action.

they failed strategically because they were unsuccessful tactically. The whole concept of the *Citadel* offensive reflected the bankruptcy of Hitler and the German High Command.'

As has been noted, the Russians launched their own offensive on July 12, as part of a plan that incorporated the German plans leaked to them by the 'Lucy' ring. The initial stages of the offensive were spearheaded by Lieutenant-General I. K. Bagramyan's 11th Guards Army of the West Front (Colonel-General V. D. Sokolovsky) north-west of Orel and by Lieutenant-General A. V. Gorbatov's 3rd Army and Lieutenant-General V. Y. Kolpatchy's 63rd Army of the Bryansk Front east of Orel. The Russian offensive was preceded by furious artillery bombardments, but German resistance was almost fanatical in its determination. The Russians did make significant advances, but by the third

The crew of a Russian anti-tank gun go into action.

day the Germans had almost halted them. Manstein, however, was forced to give up the 'Grossdeutschland' Panzergrenadier Division to Kluge.

But at this stage the Russians threw in fresh forces: Lieutenant-General V. M. Badanov's 4th Tank Army and Lieutenant-General I. I. Fedyuninsky's 11th Army (West Front), and Lieutenant-General P. S. Rybalko's 3rd Guards Tank Army (Bryansk Front). The Russian offensive once more gathered momentum. Events in Italy now once again took a hand. On July 25 Mussolini was deposed and imprisoned; and on July 29 the German monitoring service picked up a telephone conversation between Winston Churchill and Franklin Roosevelt, in which the surrender of Italy to the Allies was discussed. Hitler realised that he would need large-scale reinforcements for his southern flank in the Mediterranean, and therefore ordered Kluge on August 1 to pull back to the 'Hagen Line' – the non-existent defence line across the neck of the Orel salient. This would, it was hoped, allow Army Group 'Centre' to send men and armour to Italy. By August 18 the Germans had lost the Orel salient to the combined advances of the West, Bryansk and Central Fronts.

It was now the turn of Manstein's Army Group 'South' to receive the attentions of the Russians. As part of the general offensive that was to drive the Germans back to the line of the Dniepr by the end of September, Zhukov co-ordinated the attacks that wiped out all Manstein's gains north of Belgorod and then destroyed the Kharkov salient. The forces involved were drawn from Vatutin's Voronezh Front, Konev's Steppe Front, which had now moved in its entirety to positions between Belgorod and Kharkov, and General of the Army R. Ya. Malinovsky's South-West Front.

German attention was by now firmly focussed on the Russian advances further south, across the Mius and central Donets rivers, so the diversionary activities of Lieutenant-General N. Y. Chibisov's 38th Army on the western face of the Kursk salient were unnecessary. The real attack, which was launched on August 3 by four armies of the Voronezh and Steppe Fronts, came as a complete surprise to the Germans. The Russians broke through swiftly, allowing the 1st Tank and 5th Guards Tank Armies to push on into the German rear areas. Belgorod fell to the Russians on August 5, and despite hard counter-attacks by the Germans, the 4th Panzerarmee and Operational Group 'Kempf' were forced apart. Kharkov was liberated on the 23rd, and by the 25th the whole of the Kharkov salient.

The Battle of Kursk was over, and the Germans had been decisively beaten. The Eastern Front was in total disarray, and the Western Allies were about to pour into Italy, which was soon to defect to the Allied side. The writing was on the wall for Hitler.